Marshall Hanft

THE
CAPE FORTS
Guardians
of the Columbia

D1568480

Oregon Historical Society Press

COVER: West Battery, Fort Stevens, 1897. Mounting 30-ton gun tube, emplacement No. 2 (later Battery Lewis, No. 2 gun). OHS Collections.

FRONTIS: Entrance to the earthwork was across the rear ditch by wooden bridge and through this sallyport. Ca. 1880. OHS Collections.

The Library of Congress has catalogued the first printing of this title as follows:

Hanft, Marshall
    The Cape forts; guardians of the Columbia. [Rev. ed.] Portland, Oregon Historical Society [1973]
        55 p. illus. 23 cm. (OHS reprint series)
        Includes bibliographical references.

    1. Military posts—Northwestern States. 2. Northwestern States—History—Military. I. Title. II. Series: Oregon Historical Society, Portland. Reprint series.
UA26.N6H27   1973   355.4'5'097954   74-157802
ISBN 0-87595-044-2   MARC

The Cape Forts

IN the spring of 1861 there were no defense installations on the western coast of the United States north of San Francisco Bay. Neither sporadic congressional arguments and occasional executive proposals nor military urgings and specific reports of investigating committees had in the past forty years produced more than recommendations that there should be fortifications in the most pertinent areas in the Pacific Northwest, at the mouth of the Columbia River and at Puget Sound.[1]

All military units assigned to duty in that region since the first in 1849 had been sent there for the purpose of reducing immediate problems of Indian hostility. With the exception of the token force maintained to indicate possession of San Juan Island, the troops were so used.

The twenty-six regular army units of infantry and artillery present in the military Department of Oregon on 31 December 1860 were stationed at nine forts and two camps in Oregon and Washington Territory. Need for troops in the eastern seaboard with the beginning of the Civil War within a year reduced the number of these regular army units to two companies of the 9th U.S. Infantry, and Battery D of the 3rd U.S. Artillery. The regular army companies shipped out were replaced by relatively untrained but evidently willing units of the California Volunteer Infantry. By the end of December 1861, the total present for duty had declined from the seventy-one officers and 1,195 men of the year before to thirty-six officers and 620 men, regulars and

---

1. First official stirrings for active defense of the Columbia River occurred in Congress when John Floyd of Virginia moved in the House 19 December 1820 that a committee be appointed "to inquire into the situation of the settlements on the Pacific, and the expediency of occupying the River Columbia . . ." This led to the first bill on the subject. See H. H. Bancroft, *History of Oregon* (San Francisco, 1886), I:350. For report of committee appointed, see *H. Ex. Doc. No. 45, 16* Cong., 2 Sess., (Serial 57).

volunteers.[2] Local commanders accepted the necessity of more tenuous coverage of inland areas. The lack of coastal defenses remained a source of persistent worry.

Col. George Wright, 9th Infantry, when commanding the Department of Oregon, had reported in September 1860 to Lt. Gen. Winfield Scott the continued state of uncertainty about San Juan Island and called his attention to the unprotected condition of the coastline:

> Our whole littoral frontier is without a gun for its defense. Not only is the entire coast of Pugets' Sound and its flourishing towns and the Pacific sea-board within our limits thus unprotected, but our main artery, the great Columbia river, navigable for steamships one hundred and fifty miles from its mouth, with many thriving towns on its banks, the military post of Fort Vancouver, the arsenal, and the beautiful city of Portland, at the head of steamship navigation, on the Willamette, all are at the mercy of a single hostile steamer. This state of things demands the immediate and serious attention of the government.[3]

Wright discussed possible fortifications to be placed in the Puget Sound area, and then repeated the long-standing suggestion concerning fortification at the Columbia's mouth:

> The next point which should at once be provided with defenses is the mouth of the Columbia river. The principal, in fact the only safe, channel across the bar at the entrance admits of defense by works not, it is believed, of an expensive character. Measures will be taken to secure the reserve at Cape Disappointment, at which point the necessary fortifications will be erected.
>
> Although the most remote possession of the United States, this is destined, at no distant day, to become one of the most important sections of our country.

Two months later, in November, Wright detailed an officer of

---

2. *War of the Rebellion: Official Records of the Union and Confederate Armies,* Series I, Vol. L, Part I (Washington, D.C., 1897), 428-29, 793 (hereafter *WOR,* L). The Departments of Oregon and California were merged on 15 January 1861, each forming a district command with the Department of the Pacific which had headquarters at San Francisco. The District of Oregon included Washington Territory and Oregon except the Rogue River and Umpqua districts.

3. Report of the Secretary of War, 1860, *Sen. Ex. Doc. No. 1,* 36 Cong., 2 Sess., Vol. 2 (Serial 1079). In his 1855 report the Secretary of War noted: "Attention has been heretofore called to the necessity of fortifying the entrance to the Columbia river, and I would again commend it to attention and favorable consideration." *H. R. Ex. Doc. No. 1,* 34 Cong., 1 Sess., Part II, 10-11 (Serial 841).

the Corps of Topographical Engineers to survey the mouth of the Columbia River for the purpose of selecting sites for shore batteries,[4] and in June of the following year he invited

... the early attention of the general commanding the department to the defenseless condition of the posts and settlements on the Columbia River, as well as on the waters of Puget Sound. At this moment a single hostile steamer could enter the Columbia River and lay waste all the settlements to the Cascades, 150 miles, as well as the large and flourishing city of Portland, twelve miles up the Willamette River. Even this post [Fort Vancouver] and the ordnance depot are not prepared for defense against heavy guns. I am fully persuaded that no time should be lost; that a strong battery should be constructed without delay at the mouth of the Columbia on Cape Disappointment. . . . At this moment we are destitute of heavy guns, suitable for seacoast defense. Some eight or nine months since I made a requisition on the War Department for ... an ample supply of guns of heavy caliber. But my requisitions and warnings have remained unheeded.[5]

The reply of the department commander was sympathetic but not encouraging.[6] Subsequently when Wright himself assumed command of the Department of the Pacific, he continued to plead the cause for greater western coastal defense. Writing from his headquarters in San Francisco on 7 January 1862 to Milton S. Latham, U.S. Senator from California, he said: "I have recently submitted to the War Department a statement of the condition of affairs on this coast. On the whole we are in a very satisfactory state, provided our present status is not disturbed; but should we get involved in a foreign war our entire seacoast, with the exception of this harbor, is open to assaults." He further urged that "the united delegation from this coast . . . bring the subject before the Department of War and Congress."[7]

In April 1862 Maj. Benjamin Alvord, Paymaster, who had served in various capacities in Oregon since 1853, accepted commission of brigadier general of volunteers.[8] He assumed com-

---

4. See Benjamin Alvord to R. E. De Russy, 30 September 1862, in *WOR*, L, II:141.

5. Wright to D. C. Buell, 4 June 1861, in *WOR*, L, I:498.

6. Buell to Wright, 12 June 1861, in *WOR*, L, I:513.

7. Wright to Latham, *WOR*, L, I:796-97. War between Great Britain and the U.S. seemed a real possibility at this time.

8. A printed War Department obituary (Paymaster General's Office)

mand of the District of Oregon 7 July 1862 and almost immediately became absorbed in the problem of establishing fortifications at the entrance to the Columbia River.

His initial activity was based on the administrative work started nearly two years earlier by Colonel Wright. To Brig. Gen. James W. Ripley, Chief of Ordnance, U.S.A., he cited Wright's recommendations to General Scott in September 1860 and pointed to requisitions for ordnance for the Department of Oregon dated by Wright in the following month. These requisitions included a request for twenty Columbiad cannons. He asked that this be changed to fifty cannons, all to be rifled and of the heaviest caliber. He also reminded the Chief of Ordnance of the remoteness of the District of Oregon, of the many months needed to ship the guns around Cape Horn, and he asked for delivery of the armament to Astoria, Oregon.[9]

A few days later Alvord directed a letter to Gideon Welles, Secretary of the Navy, requesting consideration for assignment of an "iron-clad vessel of the character of the Monitor." He urged the Secretary's attention to the proximity of the British

dated November 10, 1884, announcing the death of Brig. Gen. Benjamin Alvord, retired, late Paymaster General, states that he was born in Rutland, Vermont, August 17, 1813; graduated from U.S. Military Academy, July 1, 1833; assigned to the 4th Infantry where he came to be captain. He served in the Florida war with credit, and was distinguished in the war with Mexico, brevetted captain and major for "gallant and meritorious conduct in the battles of Palo Alto and Resaca de la Palma," etc. From about September 1852 to July 1853, he was in command of Fort Dalles, then in charge of surveying a road in southern Oregon from the Umpqua to the Rogue River valleys. He was appointed major and paymaster June 22, 1854, and served as a paymaster for the Oregon military district and department until July 7, 1862, when he was appointed a brigadier general of volunteers and placed in command of the District of Oregon. He left the district in spring of 1865, and resigned as brigadier general of volunteers on August 8, 1865. "Brevets of lieutenant colonel, colonel and brigadier general were conferred on him for 'faithful and meritorious services during the rebellion'." He was Chief Paymaster District of Omaha and Department of the Platte, May 25, 1867-December 28, 1871; appointed Paymaster General January 1, 1872, where he remained until he retired, June 8, 1880, at his own request after over forty-six years of service. See Benjamin Alvord, AGO-ACP-3877 (1876), Box 401, National Archives.

9. Alvord to Ripley, 27 August 1862, *WOR,* L, II:89-90.

[4]

naval depot at Esquimalt Harbor on Vancouver Island. He noted to him that "frequent discovery of new gold fields is leading to constant accessions to the population and to the commerce of the Columbia River." He added, rather heavily, "These discoveries will make the country more inviting to an enemy, and doubtless impose additional motives for the Government to provide adequate defenses."[10]

On September 10 he inquired of the Assistant Adjutant General at Headquarters, Department of the Pacific, about what had been done with respect to the act of Congress of 20 February 1862, which provided "For defenses in Oregon and Washington Territory at or near the mouth of the Columbia River, $100,000, if in the judgment of the President the same or any part thereof should be advisable." He expressed to him a question as to the permanent nature of the proposed fortifications, and, calling attention to the requisitions forwarded to the Chief of Ordnance, he recommended the time intervening until the arrival of artillery be employed by engineers in preparing batteries.[11]

This recommendation stirred the aging Lt. Col. Rene De Russy, now past seventy but Chief Engineer, Department of the Pacific, to advise his headquarters that the provisions of the act of 20 February 1862 were interpreted to provide for permanent defenses at the Columbia River and that he had been directed by Gen. Joseph G. Totten, Chief Engineer, U.S.A., to examine that area, project plans for defenses, and to submit such plans to the Chief Engineer for his approval. These plans, including surveys, were mailed to Washington, D.C., he said, on 20 August 1862.[12]

De Russy's assistant, George H. Elliot, at about this time advised General Alvord of certain conclusions he had reached as a result of his recent survey work at the mouth of the Columbia River. He believed a site on the south side of the river two miles above Point Adams was the most important position to fortify

---

10. Alvord to Welles, 1 September 1862, *WOR,* L, II:96.

11. Alvord to A. A. G., 10 September 1862, *WOR,* L, II:112. This $100,000 was the first appropriation for coastal defenses in Oregon and Washington Territory (see note 22).

12: De Russy to Richard C. Drum, 25 September 1862, *WOR,* L, II:134-35.

Rare ca. 1875 interior view of original Fort Stevens earthwork, constructed 1863-65 (sallyport on left). Two guns on right are 200-pounder Parrotts, the two on left 10-inch Rodmans. OHS photo.

as it was upriver from the junction of both the north and south channels. Here on flat terrain only a few feet above sea level he would place the largest number of guns including 13 or 15-inch Rodmans, if Alvord could get them. At Cape Disappointment on the north side of the river the only suitable sites available for batteries were approximately 200 feet above the water. He was afraid that because of the height firing from smoothbore cannon would be too high to deter enemy vessels entering the river close to the cape. A smoothbore weapon, designed to fire a smooth-surfaced projectile at rest in its barrel, could not safely be depressed many degrees and remain effective. He therefore recommended for this place the newer rifled cannon which could be fired at greater angles of depression. Alvord passed this information on to the Chief of Ordnance, calling General Ripley's attention to earlier requisitions, and asking now for forty Rodman guns and twenty Parrott rifles.[13]

Within the following month he furnished to James W. Nesmith, U.S. Senator from Oregon, copies of the letters he had sent to General Ripley and the Secretary of the Navy, adding: "I am sure that these are matters which could be very much farthered by your calling at those offices and calling their attention to them."[14]

Alvord claimed no special technical knowledge of cannon or fortifications. When he asked Ripley for the Rodman and Parrott artillery he wrote the numbers in pencil and sent the letter to Colonel De Russy, asking him to enter in ink the number of guns he believed it wise to request.[15]

---

13. Alvord to Ripley, 30 September 1862, *WOR*, L, II:139. Cited also Alvord to De Russy, 30 September 1862, *WOR*, L, II:140. Elliot designated a site two miles above Point Adams as Point Ellen. It is not now identifiable by that name.

14. Alvord to Nesmith, 15 October 1862, James W. Nesmith Collection, Oregon Historical Society. An unsigned letter, 29 December 1862, in the same collection is authoritative in text and indicates cooperation with Alvord's request. Alvord later told Captain Elliot that General Ripley's decision to send the guns he promised was made "after a full conference with General Totten and the War Department and the Senators from the State . . ." Alvord to Elliot, 1 July 1864, *WOR*, L, II:888.

15. Alvord to De Russy, 30 September 1862, *WOR*, L, II:140-41.

Fort Stevens, about 1885. Guns exposed in firing position above seaward breastwork. Piece on left is 15-inch Rodman. OHS photo.

The artillery of his day was under slow but continuous change. The Columbiad cannon requisitioned by Colonel Wright had been in use in the War of 1812. These heavy, long-chambered, smoothbored, muzzle-loading guns were made of cast-iron in 8, 10, and 12-inch calibers. They fired both solid shot and shell up to a range of about 5,000 yards. The smoothbore Rodmans were manufactured in 8, 10, 15, and 20-inch calibers. Of recent design and of greater strength through improved casting, they were considered the best of the cast-iron ordnance of the 1860s. Available records of practice firing of the 15-inch smoothbore Rodman placed in the work constructed on the south side of the mouth of the Columbia River show ranges for this gun as great as 3,840 yards, using fifty pounds of mammoth powder to throw a 315-pound shell. Other smoothbore Rodmans of lesser caliber mounted there were fired at ranges up to 3,000 yards.[16]

Parrott rifles, reinforced at the breech by a heavy and visually distinctive wrought-iron exterior jacket, ranged in size from ten to 300-pounders. Bore sizes were from 3 to 10 inches. Thus the two 300-pounder Parrotts eventually mounted in 1866-67 on the east end of the "Tower" battery established at Cape Disappointment were really 10-inch caliber muzzle loading cast-iron rifles designed to fire a 300-pound shot 4,920 yards. The five 200-pounder Parrotts mounted in this same period on the seaward side of the work on the south bank of the river were 8-inch caliber guns of the same type designed to fire a 200-pound shot 4,272 yards.[17]

These guns were heavy and had to be skidded to their emplacements. The 300-pounder Parrott weighed approximately

16. Record of Artillery and Artillery Firing at Fort Stevens, Oregon, 1869-79, in RG 98, Records of U.S. Army Commands, National Archives. Of course ranges are, within limitations of weapons, circumstances, and other related factors, a matter of choice. No maximum ranges comparison is here intended.

17. G. H. Mendell, Armament Report, "Light House" Battery, Mouth of the Columbia River, 30 June 1867. Armament Report, Fort Stevens, Mouth of the Columbia River, 30 June 1867. Drawer 257, Sheets 9-7 and 3-3, respectively, in RG 77, Records Office of the Chief of Engineers, National Archives.

Fort Stevens view: smoothbores and clipped sod-covered traverses, ca. 1880.
OHS Collections.

26,500 pounds. The 15-inch smoothbore Rodman was nearly 50,000 pounds. Ten-inch smoothbore Rodmans weighed about 15,000 pounds; 8-inch smoothbore Rodmans were usually 8,500 pounds.

Rifled cannon were so new and in such limited supply that Alvord's request for them probably received little serious consideration. Nevertheless General Ripley included Parrott guns in his otherwise conditional reply to him on 22 December 1862:

[10]

Your letters in relation to heavy ordnance for armament at the mouth of the Columbia River have received the attention of this, and the Engineer, as also of the War Department. After full consideration of the subject, in connection with our present means of providing armament, and of the want of it in other positions requiring more immediate attention, it has been suggested to, and approved by, the War Department, to supply a portion of that you mention, viz, two 15-inch guns, twenty-three 10-inch and five 8-inch columbiads and fifteen Parrott 200-pounders with proper ammunition, &c., as soon as possible, consistently with other imperative requirements.[18]

This, couched as it was, was not much, but it was all he had, and Alvord made the most of it. He wrote to Colonel De Russy, General Totten, the Chief Engineer, and to the Adjutant General, Washington, D.C. For each he enclosed a copy of General Ripley's letter. To De Russy he expressed the hope that he would "have authority . . . without delay to commence the erection of the works needed to receive the said ordnance." And he added: "It will be wise to make good use of the intermediate time which must necessarily elapse in such preparations."[19]

He urged General Totten, De Russy's superior, "to order an officer of engineers to commence works at the mouth of the Columbia to be ready to receive the heavy ordnance promised in the accompanying letter of the Chief of Ordnance." He also asked that the excuse of the non-commencement of fortifications be removed as a cause of delay in the shipment of the ordnance.[20]

Of the Adjutant General, Brig. Gen. Lorenzo Thomas, he requested "that the Engineer Department may be instructed to take immediate steps to have the necessary works constructed to receive said ordnance." He pointed to the length of the voyage around Cape Horn and to the advantages of using the time which must elapse before the completion of the shipment of the guns. Referring to the act of the Congress of 20 February 1862, he recommended that the President order the commencement of the defenses therein provided for at the Columbia River, subject to his discretion. He also asked that the War Department prepare a request to the Navy Department for an iron-clad vessel.

---

18. *WOR,* L, II:259.

19. Alvord to De Russy, 2 February 1863, *WOR,* L, II:301.

20. Alvord to Totten, 17 February 1863, *WOR,* L, II:316.

Brig.-Gen. Benjamin Alvord, left. He commanded District of Oregon, 1862-65, and urged Columbia mouth fortifications. (OHS Cols.) Right, Col. Rene De Russy, Chief Engineer, Dept. of Pacific. (National Archives, U.S. Signal Corps, No. 111-BA-1777.)

His own letter to the Secretary of the Navy had not been answered.[21] He did not yet know the Congress had on 20 February 1863 appropriated $200,000 more for defenses in Oregon and Washington Territory.[22]

The Chief of Engineers authorized Colonel De Russy to begin construction of "temporary defences at the mouth of the Columbia River" exactly one month after this second appropriation,[23] and on 13 July George Elliot, now a captain, Engineer Corps, reported to Alvord that he had arrived at Cape Disappointment to commence work.[24] A few weeks later the *Oregon Argus* noted that "Capt. Elliott [*sic*] is now engaged in throwing up earthworks on Cape Hancock [Disappointment] at the mouth of the Columbia river, preparatory to mounting the guns which will probably arrive some time this fall. Col. De Russy is now at Astoria, looking out for a site on which to locate a battery on the south side of the Columbia, near Point Adams."[25]

In reality the problems Elliot faced to locate fortifications on this virgin land reduced, in the early period, the speed of construction which the news account might imply. There was, he explained, a great deal of timber and brush to be cleared. Roads and paths needed to be cut. Recent gold discoveries in the interior had thinned the local labor supply. He had brought a few men with him but needed more, and it was not until late in the fall of 1863 after he "was forced to increase the price of labor" that he was able to procure laborers in any number.[26] Thereafter

---

21. Alvord to Thomas, 25 February 1863, *WOR,* L, II:322-23.

22. George P. Sanger, ed., *The Statutes at Large, Treaties and Proclamations of the U.S.A.* (Boston, 1863), 12:665. (See 12:343 for first appropriation, 13:354 for last appropriation of $100,000 on 2 July 1864.) A Portland *Daily Oregonian* editorial 9 June 1863, p. 2, col. 1, noted the first two appropriations and stated Captain Elliot had been ordered to commence construction.

23. This authorization of 20 March 1863 cited De Russy to Delafield, 15 August 1864. D6640, RG 77, NA.

24. Alvord to Elliot, 28 August 1863, *WOR,* L, II:595-96.

25. *Oregon Argus* (Oregon City), 17 August 1863.

26. George H. Elliot, Progress report, 30 June 1864, D6640, RG 77, NA.

[13]

Fort Canby barracks and quarters about 1880. OHS photo (Davidson).

his work proceeded relatively swiftly and by February 1864, with labor continuing on the three batteries he placed on Cape Disappointment, he was also able to report almost one-third of the wooden scarp wall in position at the earthwork at Point Adams.[27]

Elliot's task, keeping always in mind he was under De Russy's direction, was that of building on the sites selected at Cape Disappointment and Point Adams, wooden platforms designed to receive artillery weapons of specific sizes. The details of construction which he followed were quite standard for his time and differed from others in similar places only as local limitations of terrain and availability of materials made necessary. The science of fortification in which he was schooled was very old, with disciplines well established.

Seacoast forts in the United States at the beginning of the Civil War were typically a closed work located on mainland or on an island, as close to the shore line as possible to make greatest use of the comparatively short range of guns, and preferably placed where conditions of channels made close the passage of ships. Where a channel was wide, forts were built on both sides.[28]

These forts were closed areas with high masonry scarps surmounted by earthen ramparts. The ditches about them were usually dry but were wet where possible. On the far side of each ditch there was ordinarily a high counterscarp wall and beyond this a slope called a glacis. Guns within the forts were mounted close together. Furnaces to heat the shot to a glowing red were generally nearby. Against unarmored wooden ships such seacoast defenses were very effective.[29]

The masonry scarps were attractive but artillery damage early in the Civil War quickly showed the practical advantage of simple earthen exterior slopes in their place.[30] In some cases, as at Point Adams, these slopes were held by wooden scarp walls.

27. Elliot to De Russy, 5 February 1864, D6552, RG 77, NA.

28. William M. Black . . . *Art of Fortification* (Washington, D.C., 1919),98-99.

29. Black, *Art of Fortification,* 98-99.

30. Black, *Art of Fortification,* 100.

Mid-1880s photo of Cleveland Rockwell's painting of ship being piloted over Columbia bar. Steep headlands of Cape Disappointment on left; at right Tongue Point extends to ship just below distant Mt. St. Helens. OHS.

The two sites under construction at the mouth of the Columbia River were separated by about five miles of water and were physically quite different from each other. Cape Disappointment on the north side was a headland of several bluffs rising at points to more than 200 feet, presenting steep scarps to the sea and the mouth of the river. The area at Point Adams finally selected for the earthwork on the south side of the river was slightly more than one-half mile from the ocean and immediately on the river beach. The terrain was low and sandy, so close to water level Captain Elliot had trouble with quicksand when placing the wooden scarp wall.[31]

These local differences required some variances in gun placement but the basic techniques in the work done at both places seem to have been much the same. Two of the three batteries built at Cape Disappointment were essentially guns emplaced in line behind parapets. In the third battery the guns were arranged behind a curved parapet, almost a V in shape. Only the center pintle 15-inch Rodman, sitting by itself on the seaward side of the lighthouse but a part of the battery in that area, was given nearly full parapet protection.[32] Elliot was not pleased with the work he had to do here because he felt the cape was "unfavorable for batteries, as the faces best adapted for them are turned up the river, and there are no positions near the water which can be occupied."[33]

At Point Adams he had more control over the terrain. There he aligned the faces of the closed earthwork to achieve what he considered the best advantage in fire power from the guns which would be emplaced behind them. The work as a shaped figure not unlike a broad arrowhead, pointed in its trace to the right of north. He set the internal angle of the two forward faces at about 110 degrees to permit fire from the left waterfront face and its rearward flank to reach approaching enemy vessels as early as possible should they attempt to run past the fort. By the same calculation, gunfire from the right face and its rearward

---

31. George H. Elliot, Progress report, 30 June 1864.

32. Military History of Fort Canby, in Selected Documents, Fort Canby, Washington. Microfilm, Oregon Historical Society.

33. George H. Elliot, Progress report, 30 June 1864.

Fort Canby, photographed ca. 1889-90 by Lt. G. W. Van Deusen, 1st U.S. Artillery, from slope of Cape Disappointment. OHS.

flank could reach upstream to stop vessels having passed the fort before they might reach a point which would give them protection.[34] With forward faces of almost 340 feet joined to rearward flanks of over 200 feet extending parallel to a closed bastion front on the land side, the work provided space for twenty-seven guns to bear on the channel ways and sixteen guns in the salients on faces and flanks of the bastion.[35]

While Elliot constructed emplacements General Alvord continued to seek weapons for them. In October 1863 a new Chief of Ordnance, Brig. Gen. George D. Ramsay, ordered shipped to Colonel De Russy for use in the harbor at San Francisco seventeen guns complete with iron carriages, equipment, and a supply of ammunition. He designated the same shipment was to be duplicated for Cape Disappointment but delivery to San Francisco was to take precedence. The carriages for the pieces were then ready but the guns still had to be banded. Shipment was to be made from New York.[36]

In the face of what he preferred to consider General Ripley's promise to send him forty-five guns, Alvord viewed Ramsay's decision to furnish only seventeen as a kind of breach of faith. He soon advised him of the acknowledged intent of his predecessor; and he hopefully suggested the balance of twenty-eight pieces be shipped. In addition he recommended a number of guns be placed in reserve at Vancouver Arsenal for use in any emergency. The following month he repeated his request for reserve armament, and he asked Ramsay at the same time for a supply of iron, 6″ x ½″ and 5″ x 1″, for use on the gun platforms and about the pintles (a pintle is the vertical support about when a gun carriage moves when traversed). Captain Elliot had exhausted the local market.[37]

---

34. *Ibid.*

35. Elliot to De Russy, 5 February 1864.

36. Third Endorsement, Ordnance Office, 7 October 1863, to letter, Hq. Department of the Pacific, to Adjutant General, Washington, D.C., 29 August 1863, *WOR*, L, II:597.

37. Alvord to Ramsay, 8 December 1863, 12 January 1864, respectively, in *WOR*, L, II:692, 726.

Fort Canby. Light House Battery at Cape Disappointment, ca. 1890. The two 300-pounder Parrott Smoothbores nearest camera were mounted in 1866. The three 10-inch Rodmans beyond were part of the first armament mounted on the cape late in 1864. The 15-inch Rodman beyond the lighthouse shack does not show. OHS.

On 21 March 1864 the Ordnance Office promised the guns requested would be sent "as soon as practicable"; but on 4 May 1864 General Ramsay stated that only seventeen guns could be sent.[38]

Alvord had no artillery unit in his command and had requested in November 1863 an officer of engineers and an officer of artillery be detailed for duty at his headquarters. The department commander when forwarding his request from San Francisco asked for similar detail of officers for his own needs. The Adjutant General, in turn, denied both requests, stating there were no officers of either branch of service who could be spared for such duty.[39]

Following this refusal the department commander designated Company A, 9th U.S. Infantry, then at Ft. Vancouver and under command of Capt. William H. Jordan, to occupy the batteries at the mouth of the Columbia River as soon as they were completed. General Alvord coordinated the assignment by asking for Captain Elliot's recommendations on whether Jordan should establish himself at works at Point Adams or Cape Disappointment; and he directed Captain Jordan to see Elliot "as to the proper site at which quarters for the troops should be built at both fortifications."[40] On 5 April 1864 Captain Jordan took post with his company at Cape Disappointment.[41]

By the end of May 1864 several 8 and 10-inch guns had been received at the cape. The arrival of the heavy ordnance accented special problems. A wharf was still to be built. Vessels could land freight on the beach only at high tide. Captain Elliot felt Captain Jordan should mount the guns. General Alvord believed

---

38. Cited in Alvord to Dyer, 23 February 1865, *WOR*, L, II:1139-40.

39. Alvord to Adjutant General, 6 November 1863, Townsend to Wright, 26 December 1863, in *WOR*, L, II:664, 709. Co. D, 3rd Artillery was ordered to Alcatraz Island, California, in January 1862, and relieved at San Juan Island, Washington Territory, by Co. C, 9th Infantry. *WOR*, L, I:801-802.

40. Alvord to Elliot, Hopkins to Jordan, 16 February 1864, *WOR*, L, II:755-56.

41. *WOR*, L, II:819.

View of the northwest side of Cape Disappointment, or Hancock, ca. 1890. OHS.

the mounting to be work for an engineer and sought a decision on the matter from the department commander. He was specially concerned about the labor and expense which would be involved in handling the 15-inch Rodmans, still to arrive.[42]

In August Alvord was still waiting for the large Rodmans, and he expressed some of his disappointment to a new department commander, Maj. Gen. Irvin McDowell—the McDowell of First Manassas. He wrote, concerning the general's projected visit to Puget Sound, "I have met with such poor encouragement in reference to the mouth of the Columbia, . . . the few ordnance being sent only after long and incessant importunities, that I have not been encouraged to say much about Point Defiance [which along with Gig Harbor in the Sound he believed should be fortified some day]."[43]

A short time later he accompanied General McDowell on a tour of the fortifications at Cape Disappointment and at Point Adams where Captain Elliot had named the earthwork there Fort Stevens, in honor of the late Maj. Gen. Isaac Ingalls Stevens. The *Daily Oregonian* noted the two places "were found in a very satisfactory state of progress." The writer of the account also believed Captain Elliot had performed valuable service, and that he had made the best use of the money available to him.[44]

Fort Stevens, though it yet held no guns, was considered in November 1864 sufficiently important at least by General Alvord for him to direct Captain Jordan at Cape Disappointment to send a detail of a non-commissioned officer and ten men to the post, to remain there to guard against a possible outbreak "if at the ensuing election Mr. Lincoln is reelected." At the same time he advised Edward De Russy, civilian agent of the Engineer Department at Astoria, of the rumors of hostile plots currently circulating, and of his precautions in placing the guard at Fort Stevens.[45]

42. Alvord to Drum, 31 May 1864, *WOR*, L, II:858.

43. Alvord to McDowell, 4 August 1864, *WOR*, L, II:928-29.

44. *Daily Oregonian*, 22 September 1864, p. 2, c. 1.

45. Hopkins to Jordan, Alvord to De Russy, 4 November 1864, *WOR*, L, II:1046-47.

A 15-inch Rodman smoothbore at Fort Canby. Originally mounted on a center pintle about 1865, it was remounted on this front pintle carriage in 1893. The masonry platform was shipped from Fort Point, California. OHS Collections.

Early the same month a newspaper correspondent in Astoria reported with considerable proprietary pride:

OUR FORTS

are now nearly completed. The one at Cape Hancock [Disappointment] has been ready for the guns for several months. The 15-inch gun was hauled up to the fort some weeks since, and by this time it is probably mounted. The works at Cape Hancock will mount *twenty-two guns*— one 15-inch gun, throwing a 450-pound solid shot, and the rest ranging down to a six-inch bore. Fort Stevens, on Point Adams, is nearly completed. It will mount *forty-two guns*—one 15-inch pivot gun, and the rest of less size. These two forts will mount *sixty-four guns,* while the fort on Scarborough's Point, on the north bank of the Columbia, opposite Fort Stevens, will probably mount enough to make an aggregate of *over a hundred guns*—rather a formidable defense for a river which up to this time has had no defense. . . . The works on Scarborough's Point are not yet begun . . .[46]

This news summary was substantially correct for construction as completed and planned for the two outer forts. Emplacements at Cape Disappointment were prepared to receive twenty guns in three separate batteries. Captain Elliot described them as

. . . "Tower" "Left" and "Centre" Batteries. The first is placed on the round hill on which the Light House stands, and is for 1.15″ gun, on centre pintle platform, and 8 guns on front pintle platforms. The Left Battery commands from well out towards the bar round into the anchorage in Bakers Bay. It is for 8 guns. The Centre Battery of 3 guns is designed to reach vessels with its fire earlier in their progress into the river by the North Channel than is possible from any other position on the Cape, except the Tower Battery. . . . There is a large magazine for each battery and the Tower Battery is connected with the others by a covered way. The platforms . . . are of timber, as also are the magazines and breast heights. The thickness of the parapets is in all cases 20′ and the superior slope is for a depression of 9°.[47]

The earthwork at Point Adams was designed to receive forty-three artillery pieces within its enclosure. No more than thirty-four weapons were provided however, and of these, only twenty-six were ever mounted. By November 1864 Captain Elliot had

---

46. Salem *Oregon Statesman,* 14 November 1864, "Letter from Astoria" dated 3 November 1864.

47. George H. Elliot, Progress report, 30 June 1864. Elliot at times referred to "Tower Battery" as "Light House Battery." This battery was later known also as "west" and "right." It is interesting to note the parapets at Cape Disappointment were of the same thickness as those on the waterfront sides of the earthwork at Point Adams.

First permanent buildings at Fort Stevens were built 1865-67 immediately behind the earthwork. View here toward initial West Battery construction. Officers quarters on left. Maj. Thomas H. Handbury, U.S. Engineers, modified barracks on right by joining another building to it on north side in 1889. He needed a diningroom for office force there during jetty construction. 1896 view. OHS (U.S. Army Engineers).

finished excavation of the ditch around the earthwork and had completed seventeen gun platforms.[48]

Planned construction at "Scarborough's Point," better known as Chinook Point, actually was not initiated there for more than thirty years, when concrete emplacements were built and Fort Columbia established.[49]

In January 1865 there were eight artillery weapons mounted at the mouth of the Columbia River. These, in the "Tower" battery at Cape Disappointment, were one 15-inch Rodman, five 10-inch Rodmans, and two 8-inch Rodmans, all smoothbores. Eight platforms in the "Left" battery were ready for guns. The three platforms in the "Centre" battery were completed but also vacant. No other guns or carriages were on hand at the cape.[50]

During the next month General Alvord felt it necessary to recapitulate for a new Chief of Ordnance that which had been promised for the mouth of the Columbia River. He protested the decision to send only seventeen guns and he asked again for the total of forty-five which he felt had been agreed upon in December 1862. He pointed to the time which shipment of the guns around Cape Horn would consume, and he urged too in the interests of economy that the guns be shipped directly to the Columbia River rather than to San Francisco as had been the case with those already shipped. "It has cost," he said, "nearly . . . as much to get them from Alcatraz Island, in the harbor of San Francisco, to this river, as it did to get them from New York to San Francisco."[51]

Whatever may have been the effects of personal pressures and

48. George H. Elliot, Report of operations, October 1864, D6665, RG 77, NA.

49. See for brief history, John Hussey, *Chinook Point and the Story of Fort Columbia* (Olympia, Washington, 1957).

50. R. E. De Russy, Armament reports, "Light House Battery," "Centre Battery," "Left Battery," Cape Disappointment, Mouth Columbia River, 8 April 1865. Drawer 257, Sheets 9-1, 9-2, 9-3, respectively, RG 77, NA. There was of course one vacant emplacement in the "Light House" battery.

51. Alvord to Dyer, 23 February 1865, *WOR*, L, II:1139-40. Brig. Gen. Alexander B. Dyer replaced General Ramsay on 12 September 1864.

changes in circumstances, and results of related decisions, armament was eventually furnished to the Pacific area, and some reached the Columbia River. On 20 February 1865 Brig. Gen. Richard Delafield, successor to Joseph Totten as Chief of Engineers, informed General McDowell that in the past year the Ordnance Department had been requested (presumably by the Engineer Department) to forward a total of thirty-four guns of varying sizes to the Pacific Coast.[52] Late in May of the same year he notified McDowell of additional requests he had placed with the Ordnance Department for artillery for the Department of the Pacific, including for the mouth of the Columbia River "five 200-pounder Parrott guns, with front pintle carriages; thirty 10-inch smooth-bore guns, with front pintle barbette carriages; five 100-pounder Parrott guns, with center pintle barbette carriages." Further, it was planned that Colonel De Russy should have for distribution "three 15-inch guns, with one center pintle and two front pintle carriages; eighteen 10-inch guns, with front pintle barbette carriages." (The barbette is a stationary type of carriage on which in an emplacement the gun remains in view over the parapet.) The Ordnance Department expected to ship these guns during the year.[53]

Lacking artillery units to man new installations in the San Francisco area as well as those at the Columbia River, General McDowell had, late in 1864, with the cooperation of Governor F. F. Low of California, and with the announced intention of instructing the personnel in the duties of artillerymen, raised the 8th California Regiment of Infantry.[54] Companies A and B were the first two units of the 8th Infantry California Volunteers mustered into the United States service. Company A of this new regiment arrived at Cape Disappointment in February 1865 and remained there with Company A, 9th U.S. Infantry. Company B, 8th Infantry California Volunteers, was sent to the Columbia River in April 1865 and took post on the 26th at Fort Stevens.[55]

52. Delafield to McDowell, *WOR*, L, II:1137.

53. Delafield to McDowell, 26 May 1865, *WOR*, L, II:1242.

54. *WOR*, L, II:1059, 1082. Capt. William H. Jordan, 9th Infantry, in command at Cape Disappointment, accepted commission as major in this regiment.

Construction of Fort Stevens so far as the Engineer Department was concerned, was completed early in April 1865. Twenty-nine platforms in the earthwork were ready for artillery pieces. One 15-inch, five 10-inch, and three 8-inch Rodman smoothbores with barbette carriages were on hand ready to be mounted by the first available troops.[56]

On 6 April Colonel De Russy reported to his headquarters that he had "directed Captain Elliot to proceed to Columbia River by the first Oregon steamer after the 8th instant to secure the engineer property at Fort Stevens, and to turn over the work to the officer designated . . . to receive it." Because of uncertainty about commencement of fortification work at Chinook Point, one of the few buildings which had been erected for construction purposes was required for storage of engineer property remaining at Point Adams. This left for use by the garrison organization still to arrive "a large barrack, a store-house, a large stable, and a smith shop." These were rough structures. Captain Elliot was to select the best locations for temporary quarters which were to be built later by the Quartermaster Department.[57]

That was the condition of the defenses at the Columbia's mouth at the end of the Civil War. Discussed since 1820, those defenses had finally come into being through the internal and external exigencies of that war—Union unease over Maximilian in Mexico, Confederate cruisers preying on Union ships in the Pacific, possibly hostile ships sheltered in the British naval base at Victoria, Canada. It was the eastern seaboard pressures of the same war which delayed until 1865 the installation of cannon which would provide an actual defense. As mentioned, it was not until January 1865 that eight guns were reported in place in Washington Territory at the Fort Cape Disappointment batteries; and it was nearly six months later before the first nine Rodman smoothbores were on platforms in Oregon at Point Adams. On 17 June 1865 Capt. Gaston d'Artois, 8th Infantry

55. *WOR*, L, II:1126, 1194. Also noted Post Return, Fort Stevens, Oregon, April 1865 (RG 94, Records of the Adjutant General's Office, NA).

56. R. E. De Russy, Armament Report, Fort Point Adams, Mouth of Columbia River, 8 April 1865. Drawer 257, Sheet 3-1, RG 77, NA.

57. De Russy to Drum, 6 April 1865, *WOR*, L, II:1182.

California Volunteers and first commanding officer at Fort Stevens, felt so enthusiastically good about what he had done there so far that he wrote Governor Addison C. Gibbs of Oregon:

I propose to raise the Stars and Stripes over this fort upon the anniversary of our independence and make this our first celebration after the downfall of the rebellion as imposing as will lay within my power. I have occupied the fort with my company but a few weeks yet and have completed the mounting of the guns forwarded for the defense of the entrance of the Columbia River. Upon this occasion which I look upon as a dedication of the first fortification thrown up in Oregon against foreign foes and domestic traitors, it would be gratification to my officers and myself if the Chief Magistrate of the loyal State of Oregon could preside over our festivities.[58]

It was of course fortunate there had been no attack on the river entrance during the years of the Civil War.

Both forts at the mouth of the river were active, strong for the day, and usually adequately garrisoned during their first fifteen years of life. Both were designated to be separate military posts but in fact they were frequently inter-related in such practical matters as the sharing of supplies, medical officers (though with protests), and command coverage.

Fort Cape Disappointment, like Fort Stevens, received additional heavy artillery pieces and by June 1867 its emplacements were filled with eighteen Rodman smoothbore cannon and two 300-pounder Parrott rifles. This was six less than the total pieces then mounted at the Oregon fort, but it stood high above the water, and despite the lack of fire coverage close to the cape because of the impracticability of depressing the smoothbore weapons that much, army engineers were more sympathetic toward it as a protected artillery defense than they were to the low ditched emplacements at Point Adams.

The place was renamed Fort Canby in January 1875, in honor of the late Brigadier and Brevet Maj. Gen. Edward R. S. Canby, killed 11 April 1873 by Modoc Indians.[59] When Fort Stevens was placed in the hands of the U.S. Engineers in 1884, Fort Canby remained an active military post; and when Fort Stevens

---

58. Gibbs Collection, OHS.

59. General Order 5, War Department, Adjutant General's Office, 28 January 1875, designating the change in name also noted General Canby had been murdered at "Lava Beds, Oregon."

[30]

These 10-inch artillery pieces were the first breech loading rifles to arrive at Fort Stevens, 1897. The view is south toward present town of Hammond. Note preparations to pull gun barrel off starboard side of barge. OHS (U.S. Army Engineers).

Horses moving the rifles, 1897. View upriver toward Youngs Bay and Astoria; immediately across the tide flats is Point Adams Life Saving Station. OHS.

Looking one of the 16 inch gun barrels and carriage in the West Battery, 1897. The Washington Hills show beyond temporary railroad trestle. OHS.

West Battery in 1897, showing two of three guns first mounted. Building at right is concrete mixer house used for constructing these emplacements. View is upriver with Washington headland just visible on left. OHS.

was again regarrisoned in 1898, it was initially with a detachment of Company M, 3rd Artillery, from Fort Canby.

It was however the last of the Columbia River forts to receive new armament at the turn of the century. Fort Columbia, the other Washington side installation at Chinook Point about six miles inland from the river mouth, had two new 8-inch rifles mounted in Battery (Jules) Ord in 1898, and 3-inch and 6-inch rifle emplacements were completed there during the next two years for Batteries (Frank) Crenshaw and (William) Murphy respectively. It was several years after this before concrete sites were ready at Fort Canby for the 6-inch rifles of Batteries (Elijah) O'Flyng and (Harvey) Allen.[60]

The first additional armament provided at Fort Stevens after 1867 were four of the total of six emplacements of West Battery, completed in 1898. The other two, unique there in that they were designed for all around fire, were finished in 1900. They were located west of the original "fort" and like it, they were near the bank of the river. These emplacements mounting 10-inch rifles on disappearing carriages were later divided into three batteries of two guns each which were named, from east to west, Lewis, Walker, and Mishler.[61]

---

60. Fort Columbia had been projected for development in 1863 but litigation on ownership of Chinook Point delayed completion of purchase of the fort site until after the Civil War, and interest lapsed. Battery Ord eventually had three 8-inch rifles mounted on it. It was named for 1st Lt. Jules G. Ord, 6th U.S. Infantry, who was killed in action on San Juan Hill, Cuba, 1 July 1898. Other batteries here mentioned were named as follows: Crenshaw for Capt. Frank F. Crenshaw, 28th Infantry, U.S. Volunteers, who died 28 August 1900, of wounds received in action in the Philippine Islands; Murphy for Capt. William L. Murphy, 39th Infantry, U.S. Volunteers, who was killed in action in the Philippine Islands, 14 August 1900; O'Flyng for Ens. Elijah Temple O'Flyng, 23rd U.S. Infantry, who died of wounds received in action at Fort Erie, Upper Canada, 18 September 1814; Allen for Lt. Col. Harvey A. Allen, 2nd U.S. Artillery, a veteran of the Mexican and Civil wars (died 20 September 1882). Battery Guenther, established at Fort Canby shortly after World War I with four 12-inch mortars from Battery Clark at Fort Stevens, was named for Brig. Gen. Francis L. Guenther (died 5 December 1918). Two 6-inch long range rifles on barbette mounts were placed at Fort Canby during World War II (Battery 247). A similar installation at Fort Coumbia (Battery 246) was never completed.

61. These batteries were named for explorer Capt. Meriwether Lewis,

[35]

By 1902 the U.S. Army Corps of Engineers had built three more concrete armament sites along the river. These became three designated batteries: Battery (James) Pratt, to the right of West Battery and between it and the earthwork, mounted two 6-inch rifles on disappearing carriages; Battery (Constant) Freeman, placed within the earthwork, including two 6-inch rifles on barbette carriages with heavy metal shields and one 15-pounder rifle on a pedestal mount; Battery (Elias) Smur, to the right of the earthwork, upriver, mounted two 15-pounder rifles, also on pedestal.[62]

Another concrete site completed at Fort Stevens in 1899 was inland and a few hundred yards south of Battery Pratt. This installation, named Battery (William) Clark, when mounted contained two pits of four 12-inch mortars each.[63]

Battery (David) Russell, the last of the concrete emplacements built at Fort Stevens, was completed in 1904.[64] Its location

of the Lewis and Clark Expedition, 1804-1806; for Col. Leverett H. Walker, Coast Artillery Corps, and Commanding Officer, Fort Stevens, 1906-1907 (died 29 October 1907 after leaving the command); and for 1st Lt. (Brevet Captain) Lyman Mishler, 5th U.S. Infantry, who was killed in action at Valverde, New Mexico, 21 February 1862.

62. These batteries were named for 1st Lt. (Brevet Captain) James P. Pratt, 11th U.S. Infantry, who was killed in action at Bethesda Church, Va., 29 May 1864; for Lt. Col. (Brevet Colonel) Constant Freeman, Corps of Artillery, who served during the Revolutionary War and War of 1812 (died 27 February 1824); and for 3rd Lt. Elias Smur, 4th Riflemen, who died 19 October 1814 of wounds received at Lyons Creek, Upper Canada.

63. Named for explorer Capt. William Clark, with the Lewis and Clark Expedition, 1804-1806.

64. The two 6-inch long range rifles of Battery 245, established during World War II west of Battery Mishler (used then as a command post), were significant to the defense of the Columbia River, but the barbette mounts were not really emplaced in the sense the large guns at the other batteries were.

Battery Russell was named by General Order No. 194, War Department, 27 December 1904, in honor of Bvt. Maj. Gen. David A. Russell (Major, 8th U.S. Infantry), who was killed in action at Opequon, Virginia, on 19 September 1864.

The emplacement for the battery was constructed in the year it was named, but the installation of the disappearing carriages and the actual mounting of the two 10-inch rifles, as well as other necessary preparations prior to test firing, all consumed a considerable amount of addi-

Baldwin 0-4-2 hauling rock for the Fort
Columbia fortification works, 1897. OHS.

Battery Freeman site at Fort Stevens, 1936, showing original Fort Stevens earthwork, built 1863-65. Photo courtesy Maynard Miller (Marshall Hanft Collection, Astoria Public Library).

above the beach near the south line of the military reservation was intended to supplement the fire power protection afforded by the all around fire battery at the river and the mortars of Battery Clark. In the next few years, fire control stations to house observing instruments were placed on higher ground a short dis- ·tance south and inland of Battery Russell. This elevated terrain came to be called Fire Control Hill.

During the early months of World War II, late in the night of 21 June 1942, this area was in the periphery of hostile gun- fire. One of several incoming enemy projectiles exploded about three hundred yards in front of Battery Russell, but with no important damage. The installation was in its turn on standby status. Jack Wood of The Dalles, Oregon, duty officer in charge, and his executive officer were in quarters below the battery commander's station playing cribbage when they heard the sound of firing. Wood quickly ran upstairs to the command sta- tion where he sighted on muzzle flashes far out at sea, and he soon determined his range to the target, an apparent submarine, was beyond that of his guns.[65]

---

tional time. An ordnance sergeant who came to Fort Stevens in 1908 re- calls that the guns at Battery Russell were oriented and ready for firing at the time of his arrival.

The gun barrels were manufactured in the east and shipped to the fort on standard gauge railroad trucks for which there was suitable track to a point near Battery Clark. From there to Battery Russell was narrow gauge. To get the barrels to the battery the resident engineer had to add another rail to his narrow gauge bed and push them one at time with all the power he could squeeze out of a twenty-five ton, narrow gauge, Baldwin locomotive.

Guns of the type mounted at Battery Russell were designed to fire a projectile of 617 pounds a distance of 16,290 yards—this with a propel- lant powder charge of 182 pounds. These weights and distances varied a little with changes of circumstances over the years and with intent. An officer on duty at the battery on the night of 21 June 1942, when an enemy shell burst in the sand 300 yards in front of the emplacement, has noted, from memory, that with a lighter projectile of about 500 pounds, the range of the battery was around 16,000 yards. (For news stories on the shelling of Fort Stevens area by Japanese submarine, see *Astorian Budget,* June 22, 23, 24, 1942; also Clark G. Reynolds' "Sub- marine Attacks on the Pacific Coast, 1942," in the May 1964 *Pacific Historical Review.*)

65. Wood correspondence with author, 1960.

[39]

PLAN
of
Cape Disappointment

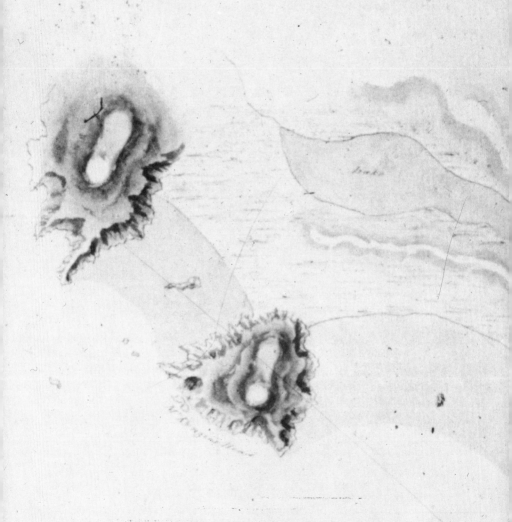

a.b.c. proposed Batteries
d   D.   Block house

Section of Warre and Vavasour's "Plan of Cape Disappointment" obtained from British Public Record Office by Thomas Vaughan. Note proposed blockhouse and battery locations.

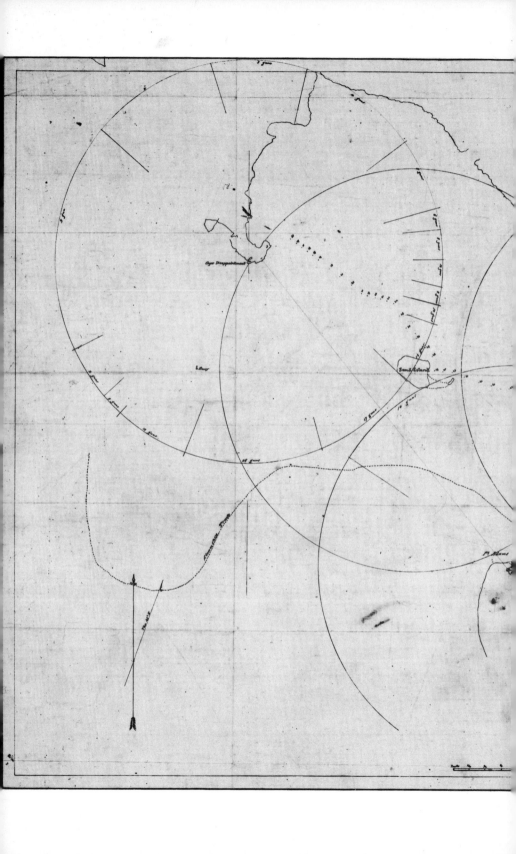

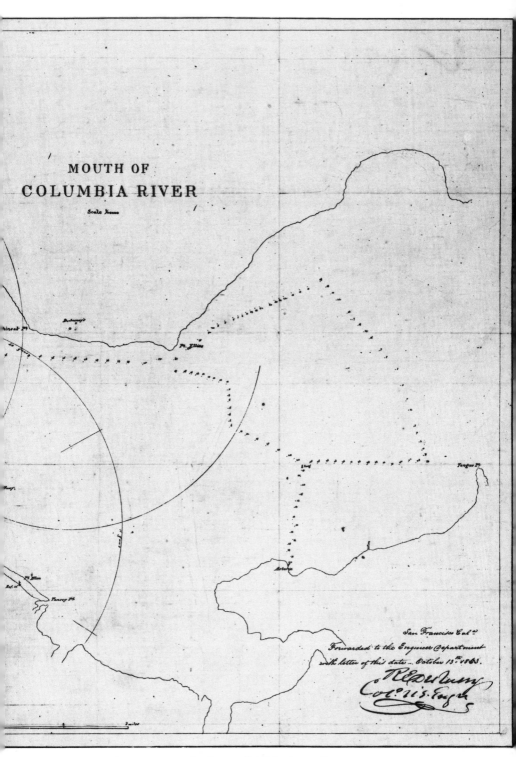

Col. Rene De Russy, Chief Engineer, Department of the Pacific, plotted arcs of firepower for guns he hoped to get in 1863 for the Columbia rivermouth forts. NA, Hanft Collection, Astoria Public Library.

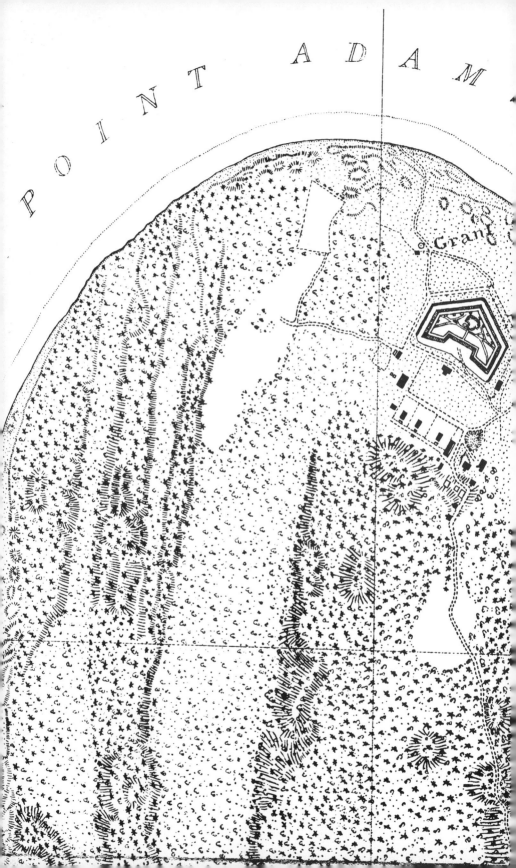

POINT ADAM

Grant

Fort Stevens, as shown in section of U.S. Coast Survey chart, "South Side of the Columbia River from Point Adams to Youngs Bay." Surveyed September-November 1868, by Cleveland Rockwell and Louis A. Sengtiller. Original at OHS.

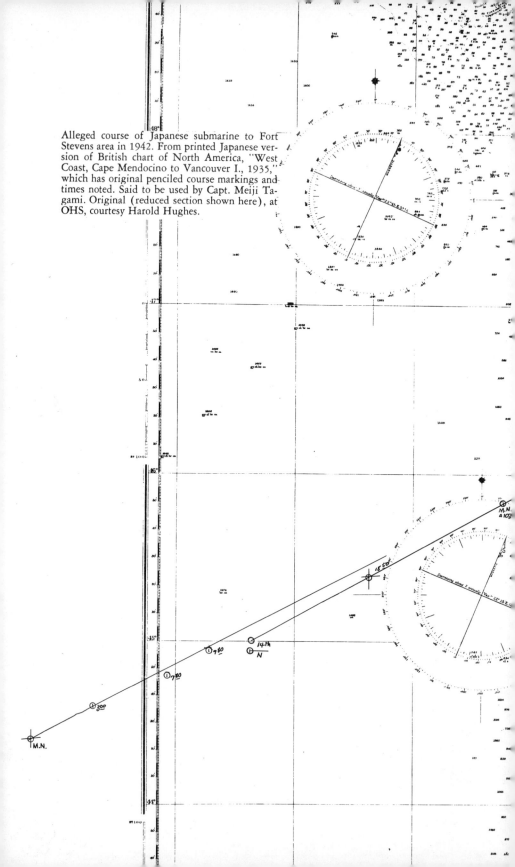

Alleged course of Japanese submarine to Fort Stevens area in 1942. From printed Japanese version of British chart of North America, "West Coast, Cape Mendocino to Vancouver I., 1935," which has original penciled course markings and times noted. Said to be used by Capt. Meiji Tagami. Original (reduced section shown here), at OHS, courtesy Harold Hughes.

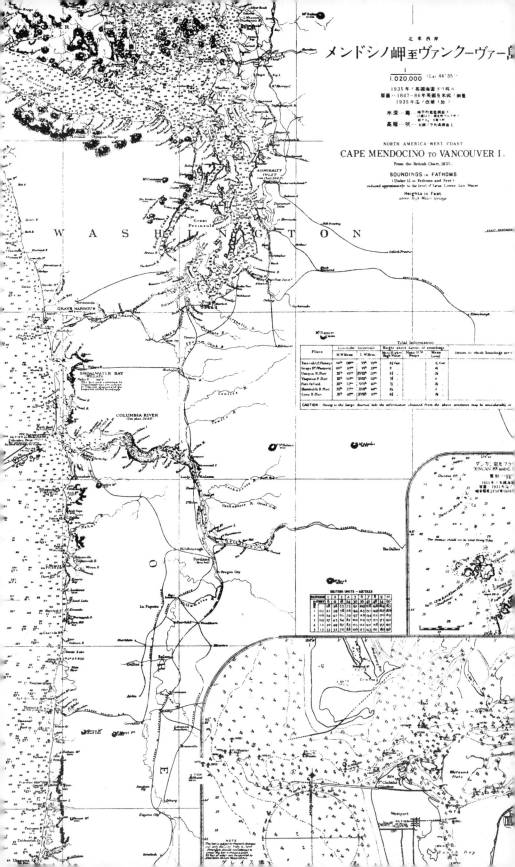

Battery Russell, 1935. Oregon National Guard at target practice, working 10-inch rifles while under a tear gas attack. Gunners of 249th Coast Atillery, Battery D, Klamath Falls. Oregon Journal Collection, OHS.

Structural plan of Battery David Russell, Fort Stevens. National Archives. Hanft Collection, Astoria Public Library.

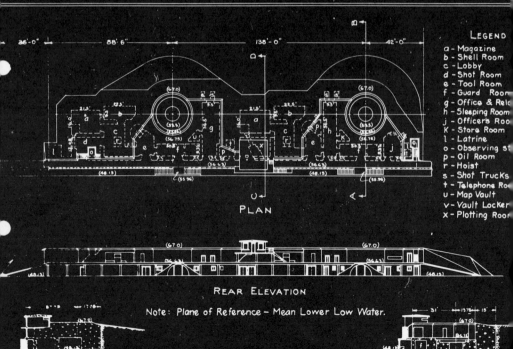

REPORT OF COMPLETED WORKS- SEACOAST FORTIFICATIONS
(Battery Plan)

Corrected to

Form 7.

COAST DEFENSES OF THE COLUMBIA
FORT STEVENS
BATTERY DAVID RUSSELL
No. of Guns 2   Caliber 10"   Carriage

LEGEND

a - Magazine
b - Shell Room
c - Lobby
d - Shot Room
e - Tool Room
f - Guard Room
g - Office & Relo
h - Sleeping Room
j - Officers Roo
k - Store Room
l - Latrine
o - Observing st
p - Oil Room
r - Hoist
s - Shot Trucks
t - Telephone Roo
u - Map Vault
v - Vault Locker
x - Plotting Roor

PLAN

REAR ELEVATION

Note: Plane of Reference - Mean Lower Low Water.

SECTION C-D

SECTION A-B

Other projectiles of a total of nine fired here generally landed in swampy ground to the rear and south of the battery. There was no significant damage to property and there were no casualties. There was understandable eagerness at all manned batteries in the defenses to return fire, particularly at Battery Pratt which was on ready status; but the choice lay with the harbor defense commander. His decision not to open fire seems to have been wise, and certainly it was indicated by the resources and the circumstances which he had. The night was dark and thus protective, and the enemy was beyond range of any gun which he controlled. To show light of any kind would have been an aid to fire direction on the vessel. He did not yet have radar.

Since the abandonment of the fort by the military in 1947, Battery Russell has by its accessibility if nothing else, come to represent to the casual visitor at least, the fort itself. The emplacement of Battery Clark can easily be seen within the fort's building area but it is now on private property. Most emplacements along the Columbia River are in a fenced area, and access there has usually not been encouraged. There was obviously more to Fort Stevens than Battery Russell, but there are qualities in the remains of that structure which attract visitors by the thousands. It has an air of solitary splendor which seems to appeal even to those who know nothing of its background.

In any case, the War Department in 1947 listed the three forts in the military areas at the mouth of the Columbia River, specifically the Harbor Defenses of the Columbia, as surplus to its needs, and disposal of certain military properties then took place. The Washington State Parks and Recreation Commission applied for the Chinook Point installations and it now operates Fort Columbia as a state park. The Department of the Army was reluctant to release or legally unable to share or pass jurisdiction on some portions of the Fort Stevens and Fort Canby reservations.

Fort Stevens State Park when established in the mid-1950s beyond the south property line of the former military reservation included no portion of the abandoned fort. The area containing Battery Russell as well as Fire Control Hill, though adjacent, was a part of 1,466 acres of the Fort Stevens Military Reservation deeded from the U.S. Government through the General

View of Fort Stevens from water tower, looking north toward Columbia River, 1906. On the left the parapet and traverses of Battery Clark, and the parados (mound of earth) behind Batteries Lewis and Mishler are still barren of vegetation. The new building in right foreground, the commanding officer quarters completed in 1905, is still in use and occupied today. OHS.

In the dead years before World War II, Fort Stevens provided a stage for practice to the 249th Coast Artillery, ONG. Here the civilian could soldier while on vacation, and he did it surprisingly well. Oregon Highway Dept. photo, Hanft Collection, Astoria Public Library.

Services Administration to the Game Commission of the State of Oregon on 21 April 1950. "The conveyance," the Game Commission told the writer in January 1962, "was highly restrictive in that it conveyed to the state the right to use the land for fish and game management purposes, exclusive of migratory birds, *only*. . . . Further interpretation of the status of the conveyance has established that improvements are still property of the U.S. Government and the responsibility, therefore, rests with them."

The writer after further study on the matter then advised Congressman Walter Norblad of Oregon of the need for federal legislation to permit transfer of the Battery Russell area to an agency which could preserve it. On 27 August 1962, Mr. Norblad introduced in the 87th Congress, 2nd Session, H. R. 12982, a bill "To provide for the waiver of a condition on certain land in Clatsop County, Oregon, so as to permit its use as a public park." It specified the area in the vicinity of the property known as Battery Russell and Fire Control Hill. The bill was referred to the Committee on Merchant Marine and Fisheries where it remained until the Congress was adjourned. It was not until 1966 that later successful congressional legislation, recorded as PL 89-452, authorized ". . . the adjustment of legislative jurisdiction exercised by the United States over lands within the Columbia River at the mouth project in the States of Washington and Oregon." This has permitted the leasing, sale, and transfer of some military properties there.

In 1967, the Oregon State Highway Department, which operates the state parks system, leased for twenty-five years from the Department of the Army 1,170 acres in the old Fort Stevens Military Reservation to add to its park holdings. A part of this acquisition still lies behind U.S. Corps of Engineer fencing along the Columbia River, but development for use is being planned. The following year, in 1968, the same state agency purchased title to the acreage including Battery Russell and Fire Control Hill, and it has extended its park services to it. The emplacement has been cleaned, an renovated to a degree; and a visitor parking area has been provided.

It is curious that Battery Russell should be that which has become a token of Fort Stevens itself. The 12-inch mortars at Battery Clark in the main fort area had been in service over five

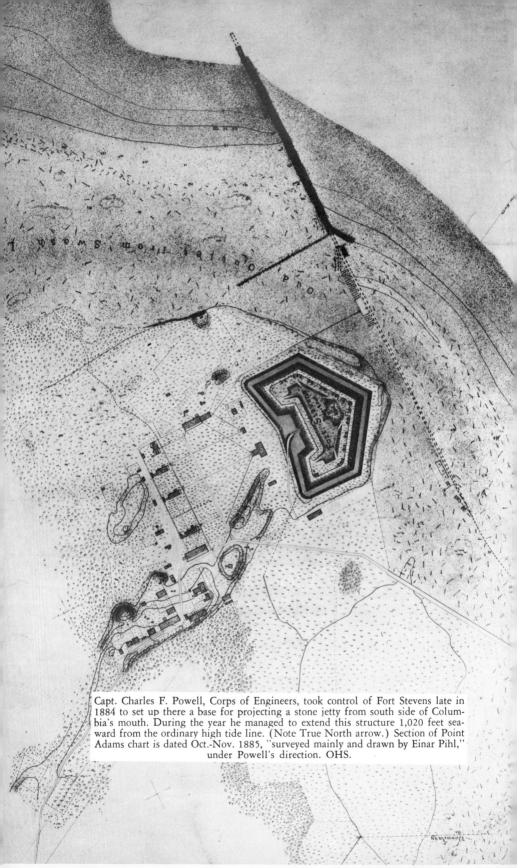

Capt. Charles F. Powell, Corps of Engineers, took control of Fort Stevens late in 1884 to set up there a base for projecting a stone jetty from south side of Columbia's mouth. During the year he managed to extend this structure 1,020 feet seaward from the ordinary high tide line. (Note True North arrow.) Section of Point Adams chart is dated Oct.-Nov. 1885, "surveyed mainly and drawn by Einar Pihl," under Powell's direction. OHS.

years when Russell was transferred to the artillery in 1904. Four of the 10-inch rifles at Battery Lewis on the river were test fired more than seven years before the guns at Russell were mounted. The 6-inch rifle emplacements to the right of Lewis, called Battry Pratt, were turned over to the artillery command before construction was started at Russell. Battery Smur, the 15-pounder rapid fire site installed to protect the mine fields, was in operation and a source of irritation to the machinists in the U.S. Engineer shack between it and the nearby jetty long before Russell could claim a gun crew.

It is unfortunate the trace of the earthwork could not have survived. Almost all the muzzle-loading cannon in it (as well as in the three batteries at Fort Canby) were sold for scrap in 1900; and the last of the first weapons mounted at Fort Stevens, the 15-inch Rodman, was removed in 1901 to make way for the modern concrete emplacements of Battery Freeman. Visible though eroded remains of the original structure remained however to clearly outline the parapets and ditch until pressure for building space just before World War II forced its complete destruction. None of the buildings which clustered about the original fort structure any more exist. The concrete emplacements and most of the buildings which are at Fort Stevens were constructed at the end of the century or in the two decades thereafter. All guns were removed from the installations there following World War II, and other metal of any value was stripped from them.[66]

Except for some surface modifications imposed by the Air Force at the seaward end of the original West Battery area during a unit's short stay there early in the 1960s, these old emplacements are substantially the same as when the post was abandoned in 1947. To the east, between Battery Pratt and Battery Smur is the site of the original earthwork fort completed in 1865. A low coast survey station tower which at one time rested on its parapet incidentally marks the place.

---

66. Armament installations at the Washington forts were similarly stripped. The Washington State Parks and Recreation Commission now controls through purchase and lease of real property more than 1,600 acres at the Fort Canby area. It has a program under way for the development of park lands there.

German naval training cruiser *Emden* fired a 21-gun salute when approaching Fort Stevens, Oregon, at mouth of Columbia River, 11 a.m., Sunday, 19 January 1936, enroute to anchorage off Tongue Point. The fort command returned salute, and Capt. Herbert C. Reuter, 3rd Coast Artillery, went aboard the ship (see his 1973 letter, below). Long afterward, enlisted men of his battery, with rather typical possessive pride made subtle parody of the event, of their officer with the German name visiting this war vessel of a foreign government about which there was a growing division of sentiment. Next day the vessel went upriver for a nine-day stay at Portland, its only port of call in the U.S. During docking at foot of Couch Street, several marchers demonstrating against the warship's visit were arrested and charged with parading without permit. The *Emden* was commissioned in 1925. Listed at 5,400 tons displacement, speed over 25 knots, complement of 534, and 3 to 4-inch armor on vertical sides, she carried eight 5.9-inch guns, three 3.5-inch AA, four machine guns, and four 19.7-inch torpedo tubes. She was beached after bomb damage in World War II, and demolished July 1946. (See *Jane's Fighting Ships*, 1939 and 1946-47). Photo from Fort Stevens dock by Edwin Bartcher, Battery E, 3rd Coast Artillery. Hanft Collection, Astoria Public Library.

APPENDIX ON THE "EMDEN": COLONEL REUTER'S COMMENT

"At 76 I am better at putting off than producing. My intentions to locate and extract from my daily logs in the thirties has been unsuccessful. Therefore I shall try to jog the old mind for my best recollections of those days, when Fort Stevens was our station. My German in 1936 and as of today is good enough to carry on a 'low level' conversation, but useless for diplomatic or technical matters. The German staff officers on the *Emden* were far more proficient in English, than I was in German. They made me aware of that in the first few sentences of our contacts. My assignment to the duty as 'boarding officer' was a matter of seniority. None of the older officers wanted or would volunteer for this task.

"The army flotilla at that time at Fort Stevens, Ore. consisted of three mine yawls of World War I vintage. They were twenty-five feet long, with an eight-foot beam and a decrepit underpowered gasoline engine of dubious reliability. The thought of stalling in the water, drifting around the *Emden,* caused me to insist on using the services of the U.S. Coast Guard at Hammond, Ore.

"The matter of a boarding party, firing of salutes and even making the visit was the subject of several telephone, telegraph messages and considerable buck passing. The *Emden* arrived on a *Sunday* and no one in the area was sure that boarding parties and salutes were proper on the sabbath. As I recall the decision to board was made in the army corps area headquarters at San Francisco. The Commander of the *Emden* made it plain to me that he did not consider it good form or proper on a Sunday! . . .

"Major [William R.] Stewart, commanding Fort Stevens at that time, was not directed to make the visit to the best of my recollection. Apparently the *Emden* and its superiors had not made it clear to any USA authorities the exact time, purpose or plans for their visit. My opinion then and now was that the major purpose of the visit was to determine the navigability by military vessels of the Columbia River entrance, the possibilities of submarine entrances and the military preparedness of the harbor defenses.

"Major Stewart instructed me to invite the officers of the *Emden* to his quarters at Fort Stevens that same day at 1800 for a buffet and drinks. This was not an official USA provided hospitality. The cost of all elements of the party was pro-rated between the five officers on duty at Fort Stevens and the work of serving fell on the shoulders of the army wives.

"The captain of the *Emden* informed me that he would have to consider the army invitation after I departed at about 1000.

"On my boarding the *Emden,* I noted that the ship was immaculate, but not one item of fire control equipment or armament was visible. Everything was completely covered and even its outlines hidden from passing view. There was no evidence of *radar,* but there were some significantly empty standards above the bridge.

"As usual at least one of the U.S. Army 1898 vintage saluting guns and the black powder loaded rounds malfunctioned, but the coast artillery crew managed to fire the required number of rounds within the allotted time.

"About three hours after I returned to Fort Stevens from my boarding cruise, the commanding officer at Fort Stevens received an acceptance of his invitation for the *Emden* officers to visit Fort Stevens. The party was on. I do not recall the exact number of officers that accompanied the captain, but I believe that we were outnumbered two to one. Only one of the German officers failed to take an active pleasant part in the festivities and I gathered from my small bits of small talk that he was the 'Political Officer,' whose duty was to report directly to the Fuehrer. . . ."

Above, officers and men at parade, ca. 1875, Fort Canby. OHS.

Right, contrasting activity and dress at Fort Stevens, ca. 1915. 1st Company, Coast Artillery Corps, Oregon National Guard (Ashland, Oregon), loading 10-inch rifle at (evidently) Battery Lewis. Photo by A. Bert Freeman, OHS.

parapet crossed material trestle leading to concrete mixer at so low a level as to necessitate a bascule bridge in parapet track. The loaded train has just come from the sand pit, a dune area occupied now by buildings which were once barracks and officer quarters. Note other trestles in background which provide for switch tracks. OHS.

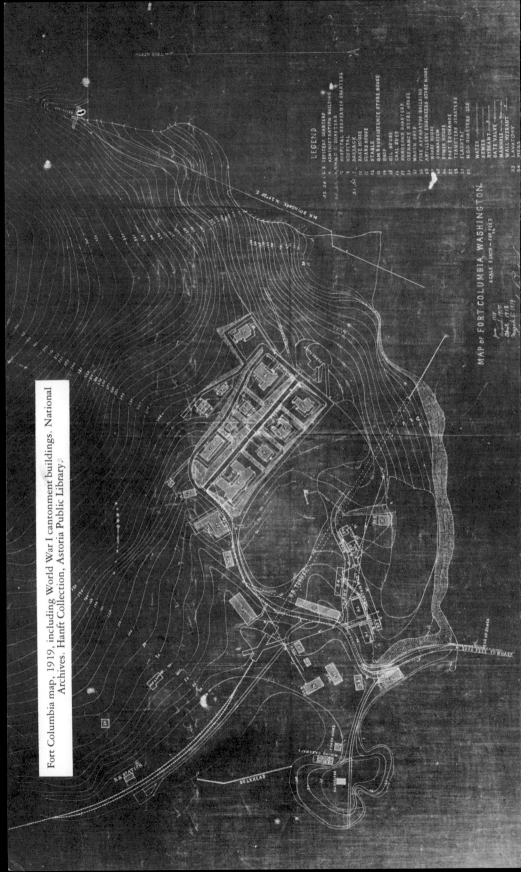

Fort Columbia map, 1919, including World War I cantonment buildings. National Archives. Hanft Collection, Astoria Public Library.

MAP of FORT COLUMBIA, WASHINGTON.

SCALE 1 INCH = 100 FEET

LEGEND

1. OFFICERS QUARTERS
2. ADMINISTRATION BUILDING
3. ANIMAL SHELTER
4. HOSPITAL RESIDENT'S QUARTERS
5. HOSPITAL
6. BARRACK
7. BAKE HOUSE
8. GUARD HOUSE
9. STABLE
10. GAS & SUBSISTENCE STORE HOUSE
11. COAL HOUSE
12. OIL HOUSE
13. COAL SHED
14. SURGEONS QUARTERS
15. ORDNANCE STORE HOUSE
16. WAGON SHED
17. FIRE APPARATUS BUILDING
18. POST ENGINEERS STORE HOUSE
19. WHARF HOUSE
20. GYMNASIUM
21. POWER HOUSE
22. POST EXCHANGE
23. TEAMSTERS QUARTERS
24. TRUMPETER QUARTERS
25. N.C.O. QUARTERS SIX

— WATER
— HYDRANT
— GATE VALVE
— MANHOLE
— WALL HYDRANT
— LAVATORY
— MESS

Fort Canby map, 1919, including World War I cantonment buildings, National Archives. Hanft Collection, Astoria Public Library.

Coast Artillery duty required more than average ability in its officers. In this rare photo, Capt. Forest Campbell, Battery A, 249th Coast Artillery, ONG, is at a transit checking orientation of the mortars in Pit A. of Battery Clark, Fort Stevens, to see if directional indexes need resetting. Edwin Bartcher photo, ca. 1935, Hanft Collection, Astoria Public Library.

A soldier always has something to clean. Here in 1930 it was one of the 6-inch rifles of Battery Pratt. Pan under the breech was to catch any dripping oil. Oregon Highway Dept. photo, Hanft Collection, Astoria Public Library.

The 6-inch rifles of Battery Allen at Fort Canby were high above the ocean on Cape Disappointment. 1935 photo by Edwin Bartcher, Hanft Collection, Astoria Public Library.

Mel Richardson, Oregon National Guardsman, gives scale to size of 12-inch mortar at Battery Clark, Fort Stevens. Bartcher photo, 1935, Hanft Collection, Astoria Public Library.

Above, view from Fort Columbia State Park, Washington, across Battery Ord emplacements, toward mouth of Columbia River, with Bakers Bay and Cape Disappointment in the right background. Battery Ord has not had weapons since World War I. Below are officer quarters and barracks. 1968 photos, Seufert Collections, OHS.